DAN COATES PLAYS EASY PIANO SELEC
FIDDLER ON THE ROOF

WITHDRAWN FROM STOCK

West Berkshire Council

34125 00 1051495

© 1993 WARNER BROS. PUBLICATIONS INC.
All Rights Reserved

Any duplication, adaptation or arrangement of the compositions
contained in this collection requires the written consent of the Publisher.
No part of this book may be photocopied or reproduced in any way without permission.
Unauthorized uses are an infringement of the U.S. Copyright Act and are punishable by Law.

22266

8.99

DAN COATES

DAN COATES is perhaps the most widely acclaimed name in the field of printed music. Equally adept in arranging for beginners or accomplished musicians, his publications have been enthusiastically received by teachers and professionals nationwide.

Born in Syracuse, New York, Dan began to play piano at age four. By the time he was fifteen, he'd won a New York State competition for music composers. After high school graduation, he toured the United States, Canada and Europe as arranger and pianist with the world famous group "Up With People".

Dan settled in Miami, Florida, where he studied piano with Ivan Davis at the University of Miami, while playing professionally throughout the South Florida area. Dan's unique piano arrangements became the talk of the entertainment field, and as he began to publish, his fame grew. In 1982, Dan began his association with Warner Bros. Music.

A very busy and talented songwriter/arranger, Dan currently lives and works in the Los Angeles area. Throughout the year, he conducts piano workshops around the country, where piano teachers and students attend to hear him demonstrate his popular arrangements.

CONTENTS

At the moment, Jerry Bock is writing both words and music for an original musical. With a book by Jerry Sterner *(Other People's Money)*, it is scheduled for the '93-'94 season. Mr. Bock is a member of the Dramatists' Guild, The Songwriters' Guild of America, The National Academy of Popular Music, The National Association of Recording Arts & Sciences and AFTRA. He is part of an endowment group in the National Foundation for Advancement in the Arts, and is about to serve his third term on the advisory panel for the BMI Foundation.

As for Patti, his wife, George, their son and Portia, their daughter, Bock confesses they are his longest running hit.

Photo: Margery Gray Harnick

JERRY BOCK was born in New Haven, on November 23, 1928. That was his first out-of-town-tryout. Thirty years later he and Sheldon Harnick gave birth to *The Body Beautiful* in Philadelphia. That was his fourth out-of-town tryout. In between was *Catch A Star*, a fleeting revue that, according to critic Walter Kerr, posed the question, "What do you call something between a flop and a smash?" Kerr's answer, "A flash". Next, Jule Styne, producer and Tommy Valando, music publisher, midwifed Bock, Larry Holofcener and George Weiss into birthing *Mr. Wonderful*, starring Sammy Davis Jr. The title song and *Too Close For Comfort* are still active offsprings.

Bock and Harnick's celebrated collaboration yielded five scores in seven years. *The Body Beautiful, Fiorello* (winner of Broadway's triple crown; the Tony award, The New York Critics' Circle Award and The Pulitzer Prize in drama, the fourth musical to do so), *Tenderloin, She Loves Me* (winner of Variety's poll of critics as best musical and citing Bock and Harnick as best composer and lyricist), *Fiddler On The Roof* (Nine Tonys, notably the citation for best musical), *The Apple Tree* and *The Rothschilds*. In addition to the silver anniversary production of *Fiddler* (from which a major excerpt was featured in *Jerome Robbins' Broadway*), a highly esteemed revival of *The Rothschilds* enjoyed a successful run off-Bway.

Since then, Bock and Harnick were triply honored by being inducted into the Theater Hall of Fame, receiving the Johnny Mercer Award from the Songwriters Hall of Fame and the Spirit of American Creativity Award from the foundation for a Creative America. But it was the award of an honorary Doctor of Humane Letters degree from the University of Wisconsin that Bock holds near and dear, for it was there he met his wife, and it was there he decided to be a composer.

More recently, Bock wrote his first score for a film, *A Stranger Among Us*. Directed by Sidney Lumet and starring Melanie Griffith, it was invited to compete in the Cannes Film Festival of 1992.

SHELDON HARNICK, born and educated in Chicago, moved to New York City in the early 1950's to pursue a career as a composer-lyricist for the American musical theater. He contributed numbers to several revues of the era including *New Faces of 1952* (the hilarious *Boston Beguine*) and *John Murray Anderson's "Almanac"* (the sardonic *Merry Minuet*). In 1958, he began a collaboration with composer Jerry Bock to write the Broadway musical *The Body Beautiful*. The team of Bock and Harnick went on to write *Fiorello, Tenderloin, She Loves Me, Fiddler on the Roof, The Apple Tree* and *The Rothschilds*. Other collaborations include *Rex* (Richard Rodgers), *A Christmas Carol* (Michel Legrand) and *A Wonderful Life* (Joe Raposo). For *Dragons*, Mr. Harnick provided music and book as well as lyrics. With Cy Coleman, he contributed songs to the films *The Heartbreak Kid* and *Blame It On Rio*.

Mr. Harnick, at one time a professional violinist, is no stranger to the realm of opera and operetta. Among his many translations, the most frequently performed are Bizet's *Carmen*, Stravinsky's *L'Histoire du Soldat*, Mozart's *The Goose from Cairo* and Lehar's *The Merry Widow*. In addition to the libretto for *Love in Two Countries* with composer Thomas Z. Shepard, he has written libretti for three operas with Jack Beeson: *Captain Jinks of the Horse Marines, Dr. Heidegger's Fountain of Youth* and *Cyrano*.

Mr. Harnick has won two Tony Awards, two Grammy Awards, two New York Drama Critics Circle Awards, three gold records and a platinum record. He is a long time member of both the Dramatists Guild and the Songwriters Guild of America.

THE STORY

THERE IS A TEVYE!...

He may not be the milkman, and he may not look like Topol, but somewhere in your community, wherever you live, there is a Tevye, the character played by Topol in the film of "Fiddler on the Roof."

It does not matter whether your village is a towering apartment block in the middle of a concrete jungle, or a collection of huts in the African bush; somewhere, there is Tevye, a man who stands out from all the rest.

The remarkable thing about Tevye is that though he stems from Jewish folklore, and the tales of Sholom Aleichem, the famous Yiddish writer, his appeal is both immediate and universal.

As a stage musical, "Fiddler on the Roof" has been seen by 30,000,000 people throughout the world, and everywhere its sincerity and humanity have been instantly recognized. In Tokyo, the Japanese actor who played Tevye declared, "We know why it is a success here, but how is it they liked it in America?"

Topol, the Israeli actor who made a name for himself in the London stage production, says "The genius of Sholom Aleichem was that he used the background of Jewish folklore and humor as a frame, to see the general problems of a father, a husband, a member of a minority group.

"All the problems and experiences that are meaningful to Tevye are universal ones."

"Fiddler on the Roof" is the story of a small Jewish village in the Russian Ukraine in the time of the Tzars, where ordinary people live, making the best of a not very encouraging set of circumstances.

Those who saw the musical play recognized it easily. The village, and the people, could be anywhere in the world.

The millions who go to see it will identify at once: Yente, the busybody matchmaker; Motel, the honest tailor; Lazar Wolf the butcher and the richest man around, Perchik, the revolutionary student, and Tevye, the milkman with five daughters. They are friends and neighbors of the world.

FIDDLER ON THE ROOF

Lyrics by
SHELDON HARNICK

Music by
JERRY BOCK
Arranged by DAN COATES

© 1964 (Renewed 1992) MAYERLING PRODUCTIONS LTD. and JERRY BOCK ENTERPRISES
This arrangement © 1979 MAYERLING PRODUCTIONS LTD. and JERRY BOCK ENTERPRISES
All Rights Reserved

Why should he pick so cu-ri-ous a place to play his lit-tle fid-dler's

tune? A fid-dler on the roof, a

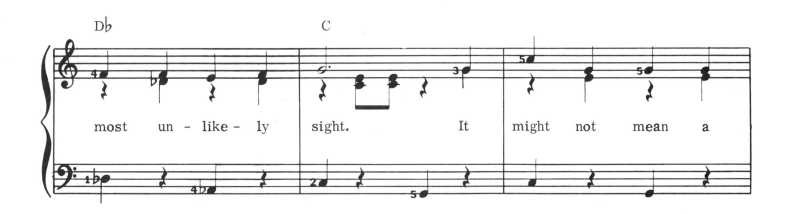

most un-like-ly sight. It might not mean a

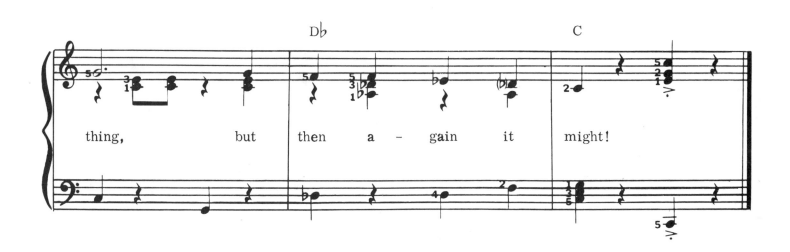

thing, but then a-gain it might!

TRADITION

Lyrics by
SHELDON HARNICK

Music by
JERRY BOCK
Arranged by DAN COATES

© 1964 (Renewed 1992) MAYERLING PRODUCTIONS LTD. and JERRY BOCK ENTERPRISES
This arrangement © 1979 MAYERLING PRODUCTIONS LTD. and JERRY BOCK ENTERPRISES
All Rights Reserved

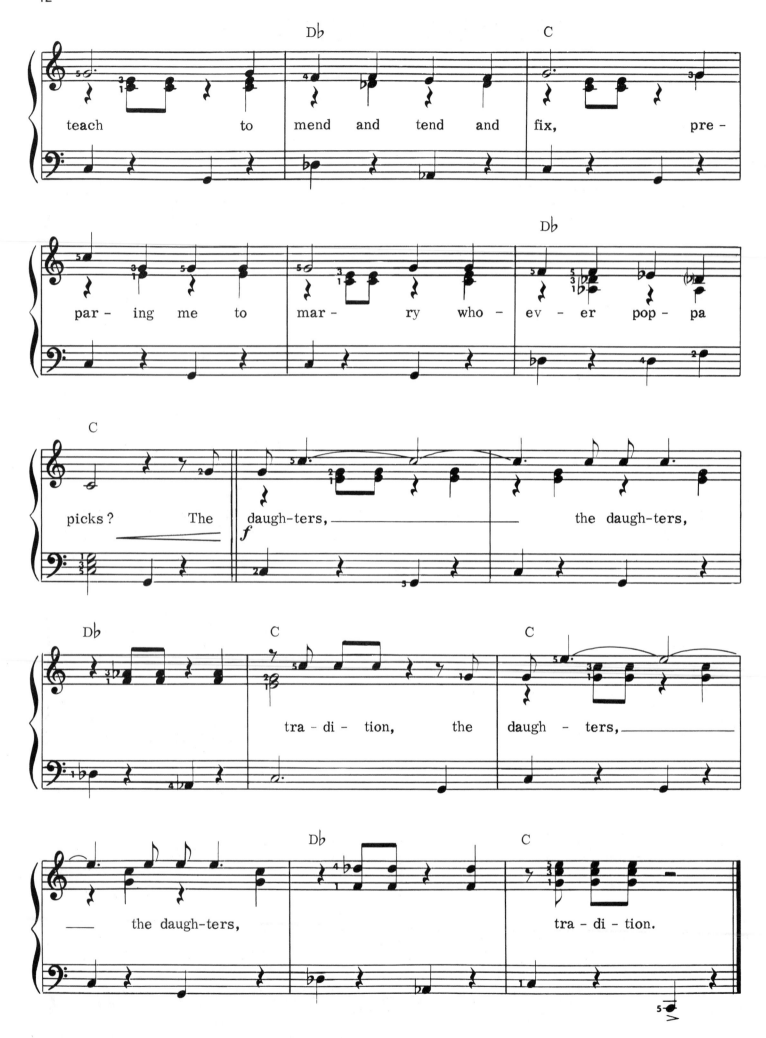

IF I WERE A RICH MAN

Lyrics by
SHELDON HARNICK

Music by
JERRY BOCK
Arranged by DAN COATES

© 1964 (Renewed 1992) MAYERLING PRODUCTIONS LTD. and JERRY BOCK ENTERPRISES
This arrangement © 1979 MAYERLING PRODUCTIONS LTD. and JERRY BOCK ENTERPRISES
All Rights Reserved

MATCHMAKER

Lyrics by
SHELDON HARNICK

Music by
JERRY BOCK
Arranged by DAN COATES

© 1964 (Renewed 1992) MAYERLING PRODUCTIONS LTD. and JERRY BOCK ENTERPRISES
This arrangement © 1979 MAYERLING PRODUCTIONS LTD. and JERRY BOCK ENTERPRISES
All Rights Reserved

pop - pa, make him a schol - ar, for
mom - ma, see that he's gen - tle, re-

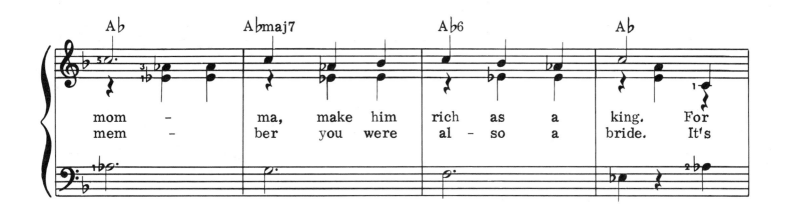

mom - ma, make him rich as a king. For
mem - ber you were al - so a bride. It's

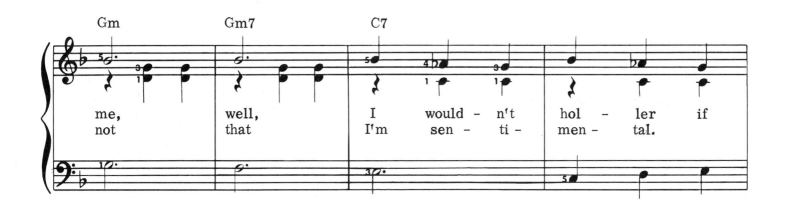

me, well, I would - n't hol - ler if
not that I'm sen - ti - men - tal.

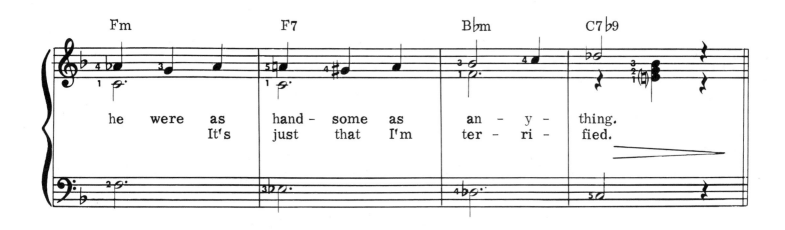

he were as hand - some as an - y - thing.
It's just that I'm ter - ri - fied.

SABBATH PRAYER

Music by
JERRY BOCK
Arranged by DAN COATES

Lyrics by
SHELDON HARNICK

© 1964 (Renewed 1992) MAYERLING PRODUCTIONS LTD. and JERRY BOCK ENTERPRISES
This arrangement © 1979 MAYERLING PRODUCTIONS LTD. and JERRY BOCK ENTERPRISES
All Rights Reserved

MIRACLE OF MIRACLES

Lyrics by
SHELDON HARNICK

Music by
JERRY BOCK
Arranged by DAN COATES

1. Won-der of won-ders, mir-a-cle of mir-a-cles,
2. Won-der of won-ders, mir-a-cle of mir-a-cles,
3. Won-der of won-ders, mir-a-cle of mir-a-cles,

God took a Dan-iel once a-gain, stood by his side and
I was a-fraid that God would frown, but like he did so
God took a tai-lor by the hand, turned him a-round and

mir-a-cle of mir-a-cles, walked him through the li-on's den.
long a-go in Jer-i-cho, God just made a
mir-a-cle of mir-a-cles, led him to the

wall fall down. When Mo-ses soft-ened Phar-aoh's heart, that was a mir-a-cle.
Prom-ised Land. When Da-vid slew Go-li-ath, yes, that was a mir-a-cle.

© 1964 (Renewed 1992) MAYERLING PRODUCTIONS LTD. and JERRY BOCK ENTERPRISES
This arrangement © 1979 MAYERLING PRODUCTIONS LTD. and JERRY BOCK ENTERPRISES
All Rights Reserved

SUNRISE, SUNSET

Lyrics by
SHELDON HARNICK

Music by
JERRY BOCK
Arranged by DAN COATES

© 1964 (Renewed 1992) MAYERLING PRODUCTIONS LTD. and JERRY BOCK ENTERPRISES
This arrangement © 1979 MAYERLING PRODUCTIONS LTD. and JERRY BOCK ENTERPRISES
All Rights Reserved

2. Now is the little boy a bridegroom,
   Now is the little girl a bride.
   Under a canopy I see them, side by side.
   Place the gold ring around her finger,
   Share the sweet wine and break the glass;
   Soon the full circle will have come to pass.
   (To Chorus:)

TO LIFE

Lyrics by
SHELDON HARNICK

Music by
JERRY BOCK
Arranged by DAN COATES

© 1964 (Renewed 1992) MAYERLING PRODUCTIONS LTD. and JERRY BOCK ENTERPRISES
This arrangement © 1979 MAYERLING PRODUCTIONS LTD. and JERRY BOCK ENTERPRISES
All Rights Reserved

FAR FROM THE HOME I LOVE

Lyrics by
SHELDON HARNICK

Music by
JERRY BOCK
Arranged by DAN COATES

© 1964 (Renewed 1992) MAYERLING PRODUCTIONS LTD. and JERRY BOCK ENTERPRISES
This arrangement © 1979 MAYERLING PRODUCTIONS LTD. and JERRY BOCK ENTERPRISES
All Rights Reserved